The Scientific Method in the Real World

by L. E. Carmichael

Content Consultant
Dr. Katherine Harris
Professor of Biology
Hartnell College

CORE LIBRARY

Published by ABDO Publishing Company, PO Box 398166, Minneapolis, MN 55439. Copyright © 2013 by Abdo Consulting Group, Inc. International copyrights reserved in all countries. No part of this book may be reproduced in any form without written permission from the publisher. The Core Library™ is a trademark and logo of ABDO Publishing Company.

Printed in the United States of America,
North Mankato, Minnesota
112012
012013
♻ THIS BOOK CONTAINS AT LEAST 10% RECYCLED MATERIALS.

Editor: Karen Latchana Kenney
Series Designer: Becky Daum

Cataloging-in-Publication Data
Carmichael, L. E.
 The scientific method in the real world / L. E. Carmichael.
   p. cm. -- (Science in the real world)
Includes bibliographical references and index.
ISBN 978-1-61783-793-7
1. Science--Methodology--Juvenile literature.   I. Title.
507.2--dc21
                                              2012946795

Photo Credits: Alexander Raths/Shutterstock Images, cover, 1; Kevork Djansezian/Getty Images, 4; Kokomo Tribune, Tim Bath/AP Images, 8, 45; Popperfoto/Getty Images, 10; Universal History Archive/Getty Images, 13; Bettmann/Corbis/AP Images, 17, 22, 33, 39; Wild Horizons/UIG/Getty Images, 18; MCT/Getty Images, 21; Jay Directo/AFP/Getty Images, 24; Mircea Bezergheanu/Shutterstock Images, 27; Ryan M. Bolton/Shutterstock Images, 28; iStockphoto, 30; Stan Honda/AFP/Getty Images, 36

CONTENTS

CHAPTER ONE

Science All Around

A police detective suspects a man is guilty of murder. She knows that he had a motive and that witnesses saw his car leaving the scene of the crime. But when she compares footprints from the scene to the man's shoes, the detective realizes they are different sizes. The man is innocent.

While baking cookies, a father decides to use chocolate-covered raisins instead of chocolate chips.

Two detectives investigate the death of man in a pool.

He predicts his kids will like the taste even better, and they do. He writes a reminder in his cookbook for next time.

These two people have something in common. They're solving problems and answering questions by using the scientific method.

What Is the Scientific Method?

The scientific method is a process for gathering information about the world. People describe this process in different ways. There are four main steps:

Observe. Scientists notice something interesting or unusual in nature. They learn what's already known about it, but a question still remains.

Explain. Scientists create a story that explains what they observe. The story is called a hypothesis.

Experiment. Scientists design and conduct an experiment. They record their results. If the results do not match their predictions, scientists change their hypothesis and try a new experiment. They repeat this process until they have answered their questions.

Share. Scientists share their discoveries with other scientists, who check whether the experiments were good and the results fit with what they already know. If so, the information is accepted. It becomes new knowledge about the world.

Cockroach Chemistry

Batteries use chemical reactions to make electricity. Scientists thought it might be possible to make a living battery using the chemicals inside cockroaches. They stapled the insects to cards and inserted wires into their bellies. It worked! Sugars inside the roaches reacted with air. It made electricity. And the experiment did not harm the insects at all. Someday, living batteries could be used to power tiny electronic devices.

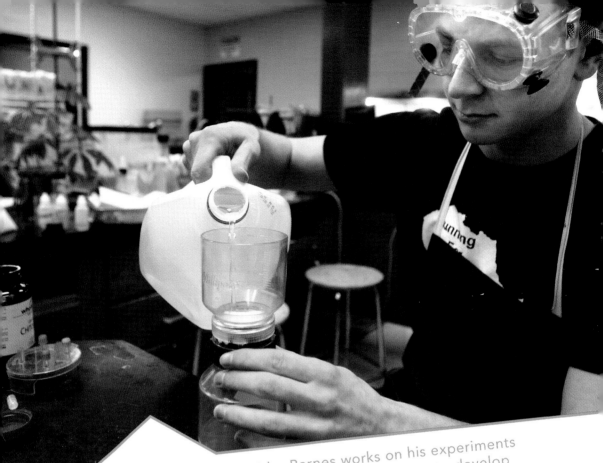

High school student Tyler Barnes works on his experiments in his school's biology lab in Kokomo, Indiana, to develop clean water and save fish in mining areas.

Using the Method

The steps of the scientific method are very important. In fact, the process is just as important as the information it produces. That's because science is more than just facts. Science is also what is done in order to understand how the world works.

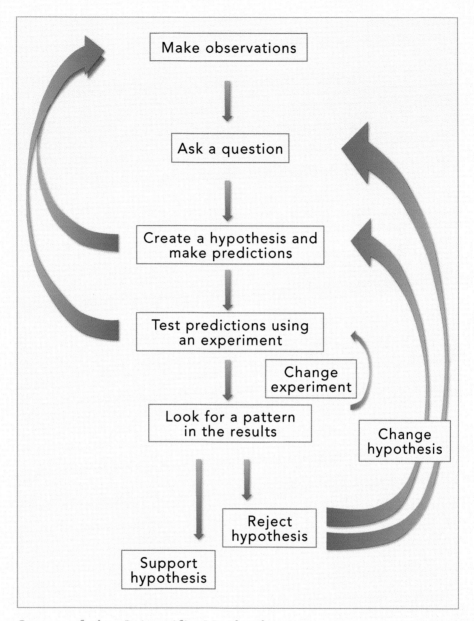

Steps of the Scientific Method

This diagram shows how scientists use the scientific method in the real world. How does the process shown compare with the method described in the chapter? How does this diagram help you understand the method? How is learning from the diagram different from learning from the text and why?

CHAPTER TWO

Inventing the Scientific Method

It took thousands of years to invent the scientific method. The earliest written record of scientific observation comes from ancient Egypt, around 5,000 years ago. It is called the *Edwin Smyth Papyrus*. This book gives instructions for doctors based on observations of patients' injuries.

The great scholar Aristotle was born in Greece in 384 BCE. He asked many questions about the world

A statue of Aristotle, the Greek philosopher, stands in the Palazzo Spada in Rome.

around him. Aristotle believed he could find the answers using just two steps: observation and careful thinking.

Scientists followed Aristotle's method for centuries. But his process sometimes led to mistakes. To improve the scientific method, new steps had to be added.

Alhazen was born in Iraq in 965 CE. He was probably the first person to add both experiments and math to Aristotle's method. That's why he's known as the father of the scientific method.

Alhazen is most famous for his experiments with light. In his book, *Book of Optics*, he became the first person to explain correctly how the eyes work.

The Scientific Revolution

European scientists believed knowledge came from reading books by ancient authors, such as Aristotle. In the 1450s it became faster and easier to make copies of books. It also became easier for Europeans to get books written outside of Europe, such as those

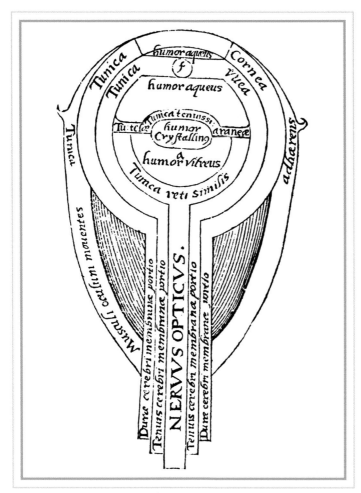

A diagram of the eye based on Alhazen's description

by Alhazen. Soon, Europeans became interested in doing their own scientific experiments. That was the start of the period known as the Scientific Revolution. Some of the most important scientists in history lived during this time.

A Revolutionary View of the Universe

For thousands of years, Europeans believed that the sun moved around the earth. In 1543 Polish scientist Nicolaus Copernicus published the book *On the Revolutions of the Heavenly Spheres*. He used math and careful observations to prove that the sun is the center of the universe and that the earth moves around it.

One of the first Scientific Revolution scientists was Galileo Galilei. Galileo was born in Italy in 1564. He is still famous for his many experiments. In 1604 Galileo decided to test his hypothesis that falling objects speed up as they fall. He rolled balls down ramps and measured the distances they traveled in certain lengths of time. He measured when they started rolling and again just before they finished.

It became important for scientists to share the information they discovered. Robert Boyle was an English scientist in the 1600s. He encouraged scientists to write reports giving clear instructions about their experiments. That way other people could read the reports, repeat the experiments, and see the results for themselves.

In 1660 Boyle and other scientists formed the Royal Society of London. The society published reports about new discoveries. At meetings, scientists showed other people how their experiments worked.

Isaac Newton became president of the Royal Society of London in 1703. He was one of the greatest scientists of all time. Newton was also interested in magic and alchemy (an early kind of chemistry). Newton was already famous for his book *The Mathematical Principles of Natural Philosophy*. It was published in 1687. *The Principles* used math to describe motion in

Scientific Magic

Magicians had used the scientific method for centuries before the Scientific Revolution. They believed that rocks, plants, and animals had hidden abilities to affect other things, such as people's diseases. To discover these abilities, magicians performed experiments and observed the results.

the universe, including gravity. Newton's book of experiments with light, called *Optics*, was published in 1704. These books not only described amazing scientific discoveries but also *how* science should be done.

EXPLORE ONLINE

The focus in Chapter Two was early scientists and the Scientific Revolution. It also touched upon the use of the scientific method by magicians. The Web site below focuses on Isaac Newton and alchemy. As you know, every source is different. How is the information given in the Web site different from the information in this chapter? What information is the same? How do the two sources present information differently? What can you learn from this Web site?

Newton the Alchemist
www.pbs.org/wgbh/nova/physics/newton-alchemist-newman.html

Isaac Newton experimented with focused rays of light.

CHAPTER THREE

Observation: Seeing Is Believing

Observation is the first step in today's scientific method. It was also the favorite step of Russian scientist Nikolai Vagner. On August 12, 1861, Vagner went for a walk. He took nothing but his magnifying glass and his sense of wonder. When he looked under the bark of a dead tree, Vagner made an amazing discovery.

Since Nikolai Vagner's discovery, it was found that salamander larvae can have babies as well.

Everyone thought that only adult insects could have babies. But Vagner saw insect larvae that contained more insect larvae. In a few days, these baby insects gave birth to new baby insects. By observing carefully, Vagner had found something that no one had known before.

The Harvard Computers

Telescopes were first attached to cameras in the late 1800s. Astronomers at Harvard University began taking thousands of photographs of stars. They hired women to help them sort through the data. These women became known as the Harvard Computers. The Harvard Computers were some of the only women included in science at the time.

Observation Across Distances

In many cases, great data can be collected with eyes, ears, and simple tools such as rulers. Other times, observation requires the use of more advanced tools. During the Scientific Revolution, two new tools were invented: telescopes and microscopes. They gave

The Hubble Space Telescope is used to take amazing pictures of space, such as this spiral galaxy.

scientists the power to observe things that had never been seen before.

Galileo was the first scientist to use a telescope. Looking through it, he saw moons moving around Jupiter. Telescopes soon became essential tools for astronomers.

The National Aeronautics and Space Administration (NASA) designed a telescope that could be placed in space. The Hubble Space Telescope went into orbit on April 25, 1990.

Scientists can see a magnified image of a mosquito's head using a special microscope.

The Hubble is used by more than 4,000 astronomers around the world. It's taken around 600,000 pictures of more than 30,000 objects in space.

Observing Tiny Things

Using microscopes, scientists could see smaller objects than they'd ever seen before.

Microscopes were invented in Holland in 1590. Hans Janssen and his son Zacharias put two glass lenses into a tube. Their first microscope made things appear up to nine times their actual size.

FURTHER EVIDENCE

There is quite a bit of information about telescopes in Chapter Three. It covered Galileo's first telescope and the Hubble telescope. But if you could pick out the main point of the chapter, what would it be? What evidence was given to support that point? Visit the Web site below to learn more about the Hubble telescope. Choose a quote from the Web site that relates to this chapter. Does this quote support the author's main point? Does it make a new point? Write a few sentences explaining how the quote you found relates to this chapter.

Hubble Space Telescope
science.nationalgeographic.com/science/space/space-exploration/hubble/

Using a small glass bead as a lens, Dutch scientist Anton van Leeuwenhoek made a different kind of microscope. His device made objects appear more than 200 times bigger.

For viewing the tiniest objects, modern scientists use scanning electron microscopes (SEMs). SEMs create almost 3D pictures using electrons instead of light waves. They can magnify objects 30,000 to 300,000 times.

CHAPTER FOUR

Proposing Explanations: The Hypothesis

A detective investigates someone's mysterious or unexpected death. The detective looks for evidence that another person was at the crime scene. Only certain types of information are relevant to the detective's hypothesis.

Scientists use hypotheses to figure out what kinds of observations might best answer their questions.

Police only record certain information from a crime scene.

Types of Hypotheses

A hypothesis is a possible explanation for how something happens or why it is the way it is. There are two main types.

A function hypothesis explains what something does or what it's for. For example: *The purpose of the heart is to pump blood.*

Ockham's Razor

When choosing between hypotheses, scientists use an idea called Ockham's razor. When there's more than one good explanation, they pick the simplest one. Simple explanations are usually easier to test. And if a simple hypothesis doesn't explain everything, it can always be made more complex.

A cause-and-effect hypothesis says that something happens because of something else. For example: *A toy car won't slide on carpet because its wheels get stuck on the fibers.*

What Makes a Good Hypothesis?

A good hypothesis explains something new, but fits with everything that's already known. *Birds can*

The hypothesis *birds can fly because of their wing feathers* is a good one.

fly because gravity doesn't work on them is a bad hypothesis. We already know that gravity works on everything.

A hypothesis has to be specific. A hypothesis must allow scientists to make predictions. Finally, a hypothesis has to be testable.

A Famous Hypothesis

For scientists who study past events, experiments are difficult or impossible to do. In these cases, observation and explanation can make up the complete scientific method. One of the most famous examples of this began in 1831, when Charles Darwin left England on the ship *Beagle*.

Charles Darwin made careful notes about the iguanas on the Galapagos Islands.

During his five-year trip around the world, Darwin made detailed observations about plants and animals he saw. His notes on iguanas in the Galapagos Islands include their appearance, numbers, food, and actions and even how they tasted when cooked!

Darwin spent more than 20 years thinking about what he'd seen. In November 1859 he published his conclusions in *The Origin of Species*. The book explains that species change over time and that these changes help individuals survive. Darwin's explanation is called the theory of evolution.

Charles Darwin wrote about the skills needed to be a good scientist in his autobiography:

> *Therefore my success as a man of science, whatever this may have amounted to, has been determined, as far as I can judge, by complex and diversified mental qualities and conditions. Of these, the most important have been—the love of science—unbounded patience in long reflecting over any subject—industry in observing and collecting facts—and a fair share of invention as well as of common sense. With such moderate abilities as I possess, it is truly surprising that I should have influenced to a considerable extent the belief of scientific men on some important points.*

> Source: *Charles Darwin.* The Autobiography of Charles Darwin: From the Life and Letters of Charles Darwin. *Ed: Francis Darwin. Project Gutenberg, 2008. 52. Web. Accessed September 22, 2012.*

Consider Your Audience

Read the passage above closely. How could you adapt Darwin's words for a modern audience, such as your neighbors or your classmates? Write a blog post giving this same information to the new audience. What is the most effective way to get your point across to this audience? How is language you use for the new audience different from Darwin's original text? Why?

CHAPTER FIVE

Designing Experiments

In ancient times, people saw that maggots often appeared on rotting meat. They hypothesized that dead things, such as rotting meat, could sometimes turn into living things, such as maggots. Aristotle was the first scientist to describe this idea. Scientists believed it for thousands of years.

In the 1600s an Italian doctor named Francesco Redi started to think that idea might be wrong. Redi

It was once a mystery to scientists how maggots appeared on rotting food.

observed flies buzzing around rotting meat before maggots appeared. Later, these maggots turned into the same kinds of flies. Redi believed that maggots hatched from fly eggs. He designed an experiment to test this hypothesis.

Designing Experiments

If maggots came from flies, then keeping flies away from meat would prevent maggots from appearing. Redi gathered four types of meat: snake, fish, eel, and steak. He put each type into two jars. One jar was sealed to keep flies out. Redi left the other jar open.

To find out if flies cause maggots, Redi had to make sure that flies were the only difference between the jars.

Avoiding Bias

When scientists start experiments, they know what results they expect. Sometimes, this makes them ignore observations that don't fit their predictions. Or, a scientist may conclude that the data supports the hypothesis when it really doesn't. This is called bias.

Francesco Redi was
an Italian doctor
and poet.

In other words, Redi tested the effect of just
one variable. In the scientific method, the variable a
scientist changes is called the independent variable.
The result of the test is called the dependent variable.
Redi's independent variable was whether the jars
were sealed. His dependent variable was whether
maggots appeared.

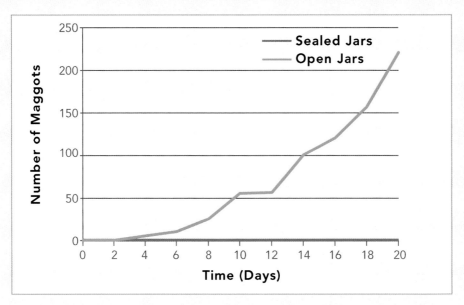

Results of Redi's Experiment
This graph shows the number of maggots that appeared in Redi's experiment. How does the graph compare with what you have read about Redi's experiment in the chapter? How does this graph help you understand Redi's results? How is learning from the graph different from learning from the text and why?

Choosing Controls

Variables that don't change during experiments are called controls. Controls help scientists prove that only the independent variable could have caused the results. Using the same type of meat in open and closed jars is a control. So is using more than one type. It can show the contrast or similarity among the different types of meat.

Redi's open jars were his control group. These jars matched real-world conditions known to produce maggots. The sealed jars were his experimental group. In these jars, he didn't know for sure what would happen.

Observing Results and Adjusting Experiments

After setting up his jars, Redi recorded what he saw. Flies went into the open jars. Within 24 hours, maggots appeared on the meat. He saw no maggots inside the sealed jars. Redi had shown that fly eggs were the source of maggots.

Redi's experiments supported his hypothesis. It's very common, though, for experiments to prove that a hypothesis is wrong. Being wrong is a normal and expected part of the scientific method. Repeating an experiment is very important. If the same results occur again and again, the experiment provides more solid proof of the theory. If the results change, it proves that there is a fault with the theory.

CHAPTER SIX

Answers . . . and More Questions

After an experiment, scientists organize their data. They look for patterns that tell them if their questions have been answered. Math is one way of finding patterns. Tables and graphs are other tools scientists use.

Scientists avoid bias when making observations. They also avoid bias when looking for patterns.

Jørn Hurum of the University of Oslo Natural History Museum displays a photograph of a 47-million-year-old fossil primate during a conference on May 19, 2009.

Supporting a Hypothesis

It's usually easy to tell when a hypothesis needs to be rejected. Supporting one can be more difficult.

It's usually impossible to include all members of a group in an experiment. But if the sample size is large enough, the results will closely match the true situation. For this reason, choosing a good sample size is a big part of experimental design. It's also important to keep in mind when deciding whether a hypothesis is supported.

Dr. Carl Sagan discussed the solar system at a news conference in 1990.

Checking Each Other's Work

Scientists write reports to share their discoveries with others. If other scientists can repeat the experiment and get the same results, the new information is trustworthy. Different experiments that all give the same answer are very convincing.

Sharing is important when results are surprising. If the data goes against what's already known, scientists may need a lot of convincing.

Cold Fusion

The sun's energy comes from nuclear fusion. Fusion can be made on Earth too. Scientists can create the conditions needed for fusion to occur by using special equipment. On March 23, 1989, Martin Fleischmann and Stanley Pons announced that they'd observed fusion at room temperature.

There were problems, however. Fleischmann and Pons wouldn't share their experiments, and other scientists couldn't repeat them. Most people decided that cold fusion was a fake.

New Questions

The scientific method doesn't end when discoveries are accepted. Most of the time, new answers lead to new questions. All around the world, scientists are doing the same thing— making new discoveries and asking new questions. And they'll keep looking for answers using the scientific method.

Albert Einstein and Carl Sagan were two very famous scientists. In these quotes, they discussed some thoughts on the scientific method:

The most beautiful experience we can have is the mysterious. It is the fundamental emotion that stands at the cradle of true art and true science. Whoever does not know it and can no longer wonder, no longer marvel, is as good as dead, and his eyes are dimmed.

Source: Albert Einstein. "The World as I See It." Ideas and Opinions. Ed. Carl Seelig. New York: Bonanza Books, 1954. 8–11. Print. 11.

At the heart of science is an essential balance between two seemingly contradictory attitudes—an openness to new ideas, no matter how bizarre and counterintuitive, and the most ruthlessly skeptical scrutiny of all ideas, old and new. This is how deep truths are winnowed from deep nonsense.

Source: Carl Sagan. The Demon-Haunted World: Science as a Candle in the Dark. New York: Ballantine Books, 1996. Print. 304.

Nice View

Einstein and Sagan are discussing the kinds of thinking that scientists use—skepticism and wonder. Which kind of thinking does each writer consider most important and why? Write a short essay explaining Einstein's and Sagan's points of view. How are they similar? How are they different?

IMPORTANT DATES

384 BCE
Aristotle is born in Greece.

965 CE
Alhazen is born in Iraq.

1543
Polish scientist Nicolaus Copernicus publishes a book proving that the sun is the center of the universe.

1590
Microscopes are invented in Holland.

1600s
Francesco Redi proves that maggots come from the eggs of flies.

1604
Galileo Galilei measures the speed of falling objects.

1687
Isaac Newton publishes *The Mathematical Principles of Natural Philosophy*, describing gravity.

1859
Charles Darwin publishes *The Origin of Species* in November.

1861
On August 12, Nikolai Vagner discovers that certain insect larvae can have babies.

1990
The Hubble Space Telescope goes into orbit around Earth on April 25.

OTHER WAYS YOU CAN FIND THE SCIENTIFIC METHOD IN THE REAL WORLD

If It's Broke, Fix It!

When cars, refrigerators, or DVD players break down, people use the scientific method to fix them. In the case of a DVD player, there are usually two possible hypotheses. The problem could be the player. Or it could be the connection between the player and the television. Checking the connection is an experiment that tests the second hypothesis. If there's still no picture, the problem's in the player.

Citizen Science

Some problems are just too big to be solved by a small group of scientists. Maybe the question covers a lot of space—such as "Where do birds go when they migrate?" Maybe finding the answer requires a lot of data. In these cases, scientists rely on regular people to help them. The volunteers make observations, record data, and use the scientific method to solve scientific problems. In the Stardust@Home astronomy project, volunteers even get to name particles that they discover in space!

To find projects in your area, Google "citizen science."

CSI: The Committee for Skeptical Inquiry

Pseudoscience means "fake science." The word describes amazing ideas that sound scientific but are not supported by facts or experiments. The Committee for Skeptical Inquiry (CSI) was formed in 1976. Its members use the scientific method to test pseudoscience claims. They investigate crop circles, UFOs, and mysterious creatures, such as Bigfoot. For more information, visit CSI's homepage at www.csicop.org.

Why Do I Care?

This book explains how scientists and regular people use the scientific method every day. List two or three ways that you use the scientific method. For example, pretend you've been given a new type of cell phone. What steps do you follow to learn how it works?

Another View

Find another source about the scientific method or one of the scientists covered in this book. Write a short essay comparing and contrasting the new source's point of view with that of this book's author. Be sure to answer these questions: What is the point of view of each author? How are they similar and why? How are they different and why?

Surprise Me

Learning about scientists and their discoveries can be surprising. Can you name the two or three facts in this book that you found most surprising? Write a short paragraph about each, describing what you found surprising and why.

Say What?

Studying the scientific method can mean learning a lot of new vocabulary. Find five words in this book you've never seen or heard before. Find out what they mean, and use them in a sentence. Write the meanings in your own words.

GLOSSARY

astronomers
scientists who study objects
in space

bias
ignoring or changing
observations to fit a
prediction or belief

controls
factors that stay constant
during an experiment

electron
a negatively charged particle
found inside an atom

hypothesis
a proposed explanation for
how something happens or
why it is the way it is

nuclear fusion
when two atoms combine,
creating energy and one
atom of a different type

observation
using the senses and special
tools to gather information
about the world

species
groups of living things that
are similar enough to mate

variable
a factor that changes during
an experiment

LEARN MORE

Books

Fortey, Jackie. *Great Scientists.* New York:
    DK Publishing, 2007.

Krull, Kathleen. *Charles Darwin.* New York:
    Viking, 2010.

Lane, Brian. *Crime & Detection.* New York:
    DK Publishing, 2005.

Web Links

To learn more about the scientific method,
visit ABDO Publishing Company online at
www.abdopublishing.com. Web sites about the
scientific method are featured on our Book Links page.
These links are routinely monitored and updated to
provide the most current information available.
Visit **www.mycorelibrary.com** for free additional tools
for teachers and students.

INDEX

ABOUT THE AUTHOR

L. E. Carmichael never outgrew that stage of childhood when nothing was more fun than amazing your friends with weird and wonderful facts. Carmichael writes for kids, teens, and occasionally adults. Her work has appeared in magazines, and her first kids' books were published in 2012.